797,885 Books
are available to read at

www.ForgottenBooks.com

Forgotten Books' App
Available for mobile, tablet & eReader

ISBN 978-1-334-47425-5
PIBN 10660869

This book is a reproduction of an important historical work. Forgotten Books uses state-of-the-art technology to digitally reconstruct the work, preserving the original format whilst repairing imperfections present in the aged copy. In rare cases, an imperfection in the original, such as a blemish or missing page, may be replicated in our edition. We do, however, repair the vast majority of imperfections successfully; any imperfections that remain are intentionally left to preserve the state of such historical works.

Forgotten Books is a registered trademark of FB &c Ltd.
Copyright © 2017 FB &c Ltd.
FB &c Ltd, Dalton House, 60 Windsor Avenue, London, SW19 2RR.
Company number 08720141. Registered in England and Wales.

For support please visit www.forgottenbooks.com

1 MONTH OF FREE READING

at

www.ForgottenBooks.com

By purchasing this book you are eligible for one month membership to ForgottenBooks.com, giving you unlimited access to our entire collection of over 700,000 titles via our web site and mobile apps.

To claim your free month visit:
www.forgottenbooks.com/free660869

* Offer is valid for 45 days from date of purchase. Terms and conditions apply.

English
Français
Deutsche
Italiano
Español
Português

www.forgottenbooks.com

Mythology Photography **Fiction**
Fishing Christianity **Art** Cooking
Essays Buddhism Freemasonry
Medicine **Biology** Music **Ancient Egypt** Evolution Carpentry Physics
Dance Geology **Mathematics** Fitness
Shakespeare **Folklore** Yoga Marketing
Confidence Immortality Biographies
Poetry **Psychology** Witchcraft
Electronics Chemistry History **Law**
Accounting **Philosophy** Anthropology
Alchemy Drama Quantum Mechanics
Atheism Sexual Health **Ancient History**
Entrepreneurship Languages Sport
Paleontology Needlework Islam
Metaphysics Investment Archaeology
Parenting Statistics Criminology
Motivational

than a pound sterling, although by possibility it may be of somewhat *more* value.

Taking the above suggestions as the ground-work of our plan, we now propose that, to save a needless expence in coinage, bars of gold duly assayed and stamped at the mint, shall be allowed to constitute the medium of cash payments for all sums above one, two, or three hundred pounds, as may be agreed upon; and that such bar gold shall always be estimated at such a given rate per ounce less than coined gold, as may be equivalent to the cost of coinage. For example, if coined gold were 3*l.* 17*s.* 10½*d.* per oz., let bar gold be 3*l.* 17*s.* 6*d.* per oz.

The same regulation to be applied to large payments of silver, supposing government should deem it expedient to adopt the use of silver as well as of gold in large payments.

The regulation proposed for the government of the local currency is, that country bankers be required always to meet their issues either in *coined* money, or bank of England notes.

THE END.

CURRENCY & FINANCE, 1828.

SHORT EXAMINATION

OF THE

Calculations

OF THE

CHANCELLOR OF THE EXCHEQUER,

RESPECTING THE SMALL CURRENCY,

WITH

REMARKS

ON THE

FINANCES AND TAXATION OF THE COUNTRY.

"The exigencies and uses of money not lessening with its quantity, so much as its quantity is lessened, so much must the share of every one who has a right to this money be the less, whether he be landholder for his goods, or labourer for his hire, or merchant for his brokerage." ... ple not perceiving the money to be gone, are apt to be jealous one of another," &c. &c. "But this is but scrambling amongst ourselves, and helps no more against our wants, than the putting of a short coverlet will, amongst children who lie together, preserve them all from cold; some will starve unless the father of the family provide better, and enlarge the scanty covering."—LOCKE.

"To think that things could return to what they were before the war, was one of the most dangerous errors that could be entertained."
RT. HON. W. HUSKISSON, 1815.

"Was it not foolish in the extreme because the paper system wanted regulation it should be abolished at once? It would be just as foolish to dash a watch to pieces, because it required regulation.
SIR JAMES GRAHAM, June 1828.

LONDON:
W. H. BRUCE, TRUMP STREET, KING STREET, CHEAPSIDE.
JULY, 1828.

THE writer of these few observations has no wish to exaggerate. He would be rejoiced to be able to believe the calculations of the Chancellor of the Exchequer correct. But he feels that they are not, and that they cannot be so; and so feeling, he thinks it his duty, although with great reluctance, to state the grounds of his conviction. For if seven, or even five millions of gold will be required instead of two, for the purpose of replacing the small currency, the effort will be far greater than can be permanently borne. It will consequently fail, and thousands will be ruined by the mere attempt, to no purpose whatever.

As little is any depreciation of the currency advocated in these pages. Experience has, indeed, proved that the Bullionists of 1819 were far more ignorant of the effects of their measures than the practical men whom they despised, and that they were wholly mistaken in the principle on which they estimated what they called the depreciation of the paper, *viz.* the difference between the standard and the market price of gold, which fluctuated with every event of the war. But the return to the old standard having been attempted, it is better to endeavour to carry it through, if, indeed, that be found ultimately practicable in a country circumstanced as Great Britain is.

Nor is there any thing inconsistent with the strictest adherence to the standard in the continuance of Small Notes, even as they exist at present, much less in the substitution of a fresh Note of a higher amount, and issued according to Mr. Vansittart's plan of 1818, on a deposit which should render it perfectly secure.

THE APPROACHING CESSATION OF THE SMALL NOTES, IN APRIL NEXT.

NOTWITHSTANDING the apparent apathy and indifference which has hitherto existed upon this subject, there is no question, which, at this moment, exceeds this in importance, connected as it is with the trade and agriculture of the country, and with the subsistence of the middling and lower classes. The Small Notes constitute the sole currency for wages of labour, in five-sixths of the kingdom; they are, by law, to cease in April next, and no means by which a substitute to the same extent can be supplied, are yet provided. This ought not to be a question of the profits or convenience of Country Bankers. They are, indeed, entitled to protection like others; but they can have no right to issue money on any other terms than are consistent with the good of the state.

The effects of this measure on the industrious classes demand *immediate* attention.

It is undeniable that every contraction, or reduction, of the amount of currency tends to raise the value of *money*, and in proportion, to lower that of *other* property,—to produce ruin and distress amongst the industrious and labouring classes, especially those possessed of small capital,—and to add to the burden of the national debt and taxation. The only individuals benefitted will be, as Mr. Locke says, " monied men," amongst whom must be classed all mortgagees and proprietors of the national debt, as well as all pensioners and holders of offices and sinecures, who, like Lord Grenville, and many others, are paid a *fixed amount* in hard money. The less money, therefore, they allow to exist in a country, the greater are their incomes, in proportion with those of others, and with the price of commodities; but there seems no reason why the working classes should be sacrificed to the unproductive.

It is clear that a paper currency, provided it be *secure* in itself, and payable in the *legal standard*, possesses the advantages of cheapness and convenience over a currency of silver or gold.

It is equally certain, that the amount of currency has been already greatly reduced in consequence of the panic of 1825, and of the subsequent measures of Government, and that much of the existing pressure on the community, and defalcation of the revenue, have arisen from that source. It is admitted, *even by their advocates*, that the two measures about to be carried into effect,—the one to prohibit Scotch Notes in England, the other to put an end to all Small Notes in England, in the next spring,—will add to the existing embarrassment and depression. The *extent* to which this will be the case, is involved in doubt and difficulty.

The *amount* of circulation to be annihilated is, nevertheless, *most important;* for upon it depends, not only the wisdom, but even the ultimate practicability, of these measures.

If the calculations of the Chancellor of the Exchequer be correct, they may be carried into operation, (for a time at least) although even then, with a considerable degree of additional pressure on the nation; but if, as *appears to be clear even to demonstration*, those calculations do not reach half, or perhaps the third part of the amount to be provided, then it may be safely affirmed that no decision of Ministers, no speeches of Bullionists, no Acts of Parliament, can carry them through. Thousands and hundreds of thousands may be seriously injured, and great distress created by the attempt, but it must fail; and the voice of a suffering people will be heard at last in the House of Commons.

Surely, then, it is the part of wisdom to hesitate, and, before Parliament separates, to examine and enquire.

First, To what amount will the small currency be annihilated, and gold provided.

Second, Whether measures so harsh and violent, are really *necessary* for the maintenance of cash payments, and for the public interest.

The most obvious mode of answering the first question would be to obtain, as in the case of the Scotch Banks, the information from the Country Bankers themselves; nor does there seem any reason why they should withhold, or any probability that they would withhold, information on a question so simple as the present amount of their *small* currency *only*.

But let us examine, as far as we are able, the calculation of the Chancellor of the Exchequer, which is as follows:—

(1) £9,700,000 £1 Notes, stamped in 1822-3-4 and 5.

(2) Deduct ⅕ of the above, probably in the hands of the Bankers, *unissued* in 1825 ....£1,900,000

(3) Deduct also the amount of *Scotch* £1 Notes stamped, and in circulation, leaving out those in circulation unstamped £1,700,000

(4) Deduct further, probably discredited, cancelled, and withdrawn, at and by the panic of December, 1825   2,750,000

(5) Likely to be further withdrawn by the 5th April, 1829 1,300,000

£7,650,000

£2,050,000

Leaving £2,050,000 as the amount to be withdrawn, and replaced by gold.

That this calculation is most erroneous, and that it was not drawn up by any one *practically* acquainted with the matter, is most certain. Indeed, the errors are precisely such as a practical man could not easily have fallen into, unless he had been a very dull one.

The first great error lies in the article marked (2), for it is certain that the reserve formerly kept of Notes stamped, but not issued, and which the Chancellor of the Exchequer estimates at £1,900,000, have since 1826, found their way into circulation. In consequence of no fresh stamps being allowed to replace the old Notes worn out, no Banker has now any quantity on hand; such is the demand for them on the one hand, and the natural desire to use them before they are prohibited, in April next, on the other, that no inducement exists to keep such a reserve, nor, in point of fact, does it exist.

The second error consists in deducting £1,300,000 for Notes *likely to be worn out by the 5th of April,* 1829; for the question is not what will remain in circulation at that time, but the amount in circulation *now.*

The third error consists in omitting altogether the £1 Notes of the Bank of England, and which equally come under the same prohibition.

The fourth error is in wholly omitting the extra quantity of gold, which every country Banker must keep by him, to meet his *larger* Notes, which he now generally pays in his own *small* Notes, gold being scarcely ever demanded, or wished for by the public.

Taking into account the circumstances, the calculation will probably stand nearly as follows:—

9,700,000, amount of £1 Notes stamped in 1822-3-4-5,
450,000, add for Bank of England £1 Notes.

10,150,000.
    Deduct for Scotch Notes as before 1,700,000
    Deduct for cancelled and worn out
     by, and since, the panic, &c, 2,750,000
    Deduct additional, probably worn
     out since, to this time, instead of
     1,300,000 650,000
5,100,000 ──────────────────────────

5,050,000 Notes now in circulation.
2,100,000 { Add for additional quantity of gold to be kept by the country Bankers, say 600 Banks, at £3500 each, on an average.

7,150,000 { Amount of extra quantity of gold to be drawn out of the Bank of England.

This calculation is upon the data given by the Chancellor of the Exchequer, and it is corroborated by other modes of considering the subject.—

Take, for example, six hundred Banks, at only £9000 each, and the result is £5,400,000 of small Notes in circulation. There are many Banks which have more than four times that amount yet out, and it must be indeed a small establishment which does not equal the above named sum.

Consider further, that with the exception of the Metropolis, and a part of the adjacent counties, and a *part* of Lancashire; all England, including the great counties of York, Lincoln, Devon, and Cornwall, have little or no other species of small circulation.

It is, indeed, true that the Chancellor of the Exchequer fortifies his calculation by *assuming* that, in April 1829, there would be no Notes in circulation older than January

1825. Nothing can be more erroneous than this assumption. If inquiry were to be made, it would be found that Notes dated as far back as 1820, and even further still, are yet in constant and frequent circulation.

These details are dry and uninviting, but MOST IMPORTANT.—That the calculation which has deceived the Chancellor of the Exchequer, and, through him, the House of Commons, is totally and widely incorrect, the slightest practical inquiry *on the points above referred to*, will satisfy him. He will at once discover, that nearly the whole of the £1,900,000, and the greater part of the £1,300,000, ought not to have been *deducted;* and that he ought to *add* the amount of the small Notes of the Bank of England, and the additional stock of gold which must be kept in the drawers of the country Banker.

Here, then, let the Government pause. Let them ask if *seven* additional millions of gold could be *safely* and *permanently* spared by the Bank of England. Let them ask, in this case, how that Bank would stand in the event of another panic; and let them reflect that the panic of 1793 existed when there were *no one pound Notes*, and that the panic of 1825 was stopped in its career, by an issue of Notes of *that description.*

It is here necessary to advert to another and very dangerous calculation of the Chancellor of the Exchequer; viz. that there are about twenty-two millions of Sovereigns in circulation at the present time; a calculation which does not appear to have even the shadow of a foundation. For on what does it proceed? *On the amount coined at at the Mint.*—Now, when it is considered that the exchanges have, since that period, been considerably and frequently against this country, and that the Sovereign may now be lawfully exported, and is a new and perfect coin, without the deduction even of seignorage; how can any one say what proportion has left this country, without returning, either in the pockets of travellers and smugglers, or for the purpose of balancing the exchange; or has been melted down abroad, or at home, for purposes of use or of ornament? But admitting that Sovereigns will supply the place of the paper, and that there are plenty in the coffers of the Bank, still it is obvious that the Country Banker can only procure them by paying for them in Bank Notes; to obtain which he must sell property, or *draw in advances*, or do both.

That the prohibition to issue small Notes after April next, will reduce the amount of currency, and consequently add to the existing embarrasment, to a degree far beyond the ideas of the Government, appears certain from this consideration:—The Country Banker must, in common prudence, prepare to pay off all his small Notes in a short time. As in general he does not keep more money at command than is necessary for the safety of his concern, he can only do this by selling fixed property, or by recalling advances he has made in his district, to individuals who will be obliged to meet this extraordinary, and, in most cases, unexpected demand, by a sacrifice of the whole or part of their corn, machinery, or stock in trade. As these sales will come nearly at the same time, and as no new capital will be created in lieu of that which is to be cancelled, the buyers will not be in proportion to the sellers, and a proportionate sacrifice must take place. How many industrious individuals will be ruined or destroyed, it is difficult to say; *nor will the depression be temporary.* It will extend over many years, and it will fall on those who are already incumbered, and least able to bear it. Scotland and Ireland are excluded from the above calculations, because, fortunately for them, their representatives acted with spirit and with union. Thus half the evil has been postponed, not averted; for there exists a secret party of cold calculating political economists, who will never be satisfied until they have subjected every portion of the British Empire to their dominion. "Divide et impera" is their motto, and they seem likely to succeed.

It may be asked, does there exist a real necessity for so harsh a measure: 1st, either for the security of cash payments, or, 2d, for the public safety and credit.

Why the existence of one pound Notes, payable in specie on demand, should make cash payments more insecure than they would be with £5 Notes; and why their circulation is not *equally* dangerous in this view in Scotland and Ireland as in England, no man can say. But, in point of fact, the circulation of Sovereigns renders cash-payment *less* secure and easy, instead of being *more* so; for it withdraws them from the Bank of England, which is thus, in the event of a panic, left with half the treasure which it ought to be able to bring to bear against a sudden demand for the larger Notes.

To illustrate this, we will suppose that, at the last panic, the place of the small Notes had been previously supplied by Sovereigns from the Bank,—the quantity which would have remained there, would have been utterly inadequate to meet the demand for the large Notes, and the bank must infallibly have stopped payment.

So true is this principle, that the plan of the late Mr. Ricardo, by which gold would have formed no part of the circulation, and the legal tender would have been in bars of gold by the Bank, is probably the *only one* by which the system of cash-payments can, for any length of time, be kept up in this country.

There are indeed two objections only, which have been advanced with any colour of reason against the small Notes, viz.—

That they drive out of circulation a gold coin of a similar amount;

And that their insecurity has caused much distress to the lower classes, amongst whom they chiefly circulate.

That these objections are greatly exaggerated, is clear, when we reflect that, in a considerable portion both of Lancashire, and of the home counties, Sovereigns and one pound Notes circulate indiscriminately; and that this was long the case whilst the Bank of England continued to issue small Notes.

And, with reference to their insecurity, it ought to be known, that out of 770 country Banks, 63 only stopped payment; that out of that number, 23 have since paid in full, and 31 are now making arrangements; and that those who failed by the late panic, have, upon the average, paid a dividend, of 17s. 6d. in the pound. But whatever weight there may be in these objections, they may be easily obviated by the following plan:—

PLAN PROPOSED.

That such persons as think proper to deposit security with Government, according to the principle laid down in the Bill brought into Parliament by Mr. Vansittart, in 1818, be permitted to issue Notes of £2, or £3, at their option.

The details of that Bill may be easily modified and improved. Its principle is excellent; *viz.* that security to the satisfaction of Commissioners shall be deposited for every small Note; such security to be returned for an equal value of Notes paid, and that in the mean time such Notes shall bear the stamp of security by such deposit. The expense of the Commissioners to be discharged by a small per centage on the Notes.

To such Notes what objection can exist? They would be a cheap and a secure currency. Being of a higher amount than the Sovereign, they could not drive it from circulation. They would mitigate much of the pressure and misery which must otherwise take place.

If it be said that this plan would give the holder of a

small Note an advantage in security over the holder of a large one, it may be replied, that the latter is better able to judge of the credit of a Banking Establishment than the former, and at all events that he will not be in a worse situation than by the law, which compels the payment in full *of all the small Notes* without exception.

If it be said that they will be issued to excess, it may be replied, that the deposit of security, will effectually prevent their being issued for the purpose of raising a speculative capital, and will throw the issue into the hands only of solid establishments.

If it be contended, that on such terms few persons would issue Notes at all, it may be replied, that those who decline issuing them are not injured by the measure; that in all probability a sufficient amount would be issued by respectable houses, for the sake of the legitimate profit and convenience which they would occasion, and that, at all events, in the mean time, the small Notes *now in circulation might very safely be permitted to be re-issued, for the short period during which they would last.*

And it would be a further and great advantage, that the amount in circulation, from time to time, would be accurately known to commissioners, and to the Government.

These remarks are worthy of the serious consideration of a paternal Government, which does not wish to sacrifice the debtor to the creditor, either national or private. Let it be remembered, that whoever urges the extinction of the small paper currency, urges, under the specious disguise of " sound principles," and " public faith," the increase of the national debt, the increase of the taxes, the augmentation of every sinecure, pension, and salary, and of every public and private debt and incumbrance in the kingdom. If, in 1819, Mr. Peel had in so many words proposed to add 300 millions to the national debt, did this, if there be any truth in the principles of the Bullionists; and yet he believed, and possibly still believes, himself to have been, on that occasion, a public benefactor.

Many other interesting questions will soon demand the consideration of a Government which claims and desires to be just, consistent, wise, and benevolent.

It may well be asked, whether it would not be wise to re-impose some of the taxes which were taken off in the last few years, *viz.* those on spirituous liquors, wine, silk, leather, tobacco, &c. &c.

Whether those taxes were not chiefly on luxuries, and could therefore be *easily* borne? Whether some of them were not *pernicious* luxuries; and whether, in particular, the increased consumption of gin has not, at the same time, injured agriculture, by decreasing the consumption of beer, as well as demoralized the people?

Whether the consumer has profited, as he ought, by the repeal of these taxes? Whether it would not be wiser in every view, and more justly popular, to repeal all the few remaining direct assessed taxes, such as those on windows, &c.; and thus to consult the health and ornament of the country, and get rid of surcharges, appeals, &c. &c.?

Whether the re-imposition of these taxes, or a portion of them, would not form the means of strengthening the Government in the eyes of foreign nations, and of upholding the sinking fund without adding to the national debt?

Whether the nation is not bound to keep up a *real* sinking fund, both by pledges direct, and indirect, and by the example of the wisest and most enlightened of foreign nations? To the credit of this fund is to be ascribed the low rate at which this country was able to borrow money in the late war, and the great reductions in the 5 and 4 per cents. made since the peace.

Why Ireland should have the liberty of exporting her poor, and her produce, duty free, to Great Britain, and yet be exempt from land tax, small tithe, and poor's rate?

To what end we continue a system of policy, which thus enables the absentee Irish land-owner, to extract to himself more of the produce of the land, than the land-owner of this or any other country, and that at the expense and to the injury of Great Britain?

Why the right to take tithe in kind in England is not commuted for an annual payment, varying with the price of corn; and the annoyance of the present system thus for ever removed?

If political economists would apply themselves to what is useful, and practicable, they might render themselves as great a blessing to the country, as they have of late years been the reverse.

THE END.

HINTS

ON

POLITICAL ECONOMY,

IN

TWO LETTERS,

TO

COUNTRY BANKERS,

AND THE

LANDED INTEREST.

BY

—— WRIGHT, ESQR.

Nottingham:

THE JOURNAL OFFICE, BY G. STRETTON.

1828.

No. IV.—Prices of Gold and Silver, and Exchanges on Hamburg and Paris, to February, 1819, extracted from the Appendix to the Second Report of the Secret Committee on the expediency of the Bank resuming Cash Payments; the quotations after February, 1819, are from Lloyd's Lists.

Date.	Price of Standard Gold in Bars per oz.	Price of Standard Silver per oz.	Price of Spanish Dollars per oz.	Exchange on Hamburg. 2½ usance.	Exchange on Paris. 1 day's date.
	£. s. d.	s. d	s. d.		
1797 Feb. 24	3 17 6	5 5	5 3½	36. 0	—
Aug. 25	3 17 6	5 2	5 0	37. 7	—
1798 Feb. 23	3 17 10½	—	4 11½	38. 0	—
Aug. 24	3 17 10½	5 1	5 0	37. 3	—
1799 Feb. 22	3 17 9	—	5 1	37. 7	—
Aug. 23	3 17 9	—	5 2½	34. 0	—
1800 Feb. 28	—	—	5 7	31. 4	—
Aug. 22	4 5 0 F	—	5 7	32. 2	—
1801 Feb. 27	4 4 0 F	—	5 10	31. 7	—
Aug. 25	—	—	5 10	31. 6	—
1802 Feb. 26	4 3 6 F	5 11½	5 9	32. 2	—
Aug. 27	—	5 6	5 3½	33. 2	23.10
1803 Feb. 25	—	5 7½	5 5	34. 4	24. 8
Aug. 26	—	—	—	32.10	23.16
1804 Feb. 24	—	—	5 7	34. 8	24.14
Aug. 31	4 0 0	—	5 1½	35.10	25. 4
Oct. 19	4 0 0	—	5 0	35. 8	25. 2
1805 Feb. 26	4 0 0	—	5 4	35. 8	25.12
Aug. 27	4 0 0	—	5 3½	35. 5	25.12
Nov. 26	—	5 9½	5 7	32. 9	25. 4
1806 Feb. 25	—	—	—	34. 2	24.12
Aug. 26	—	—	—	34. 5	24. 7
1807 Feb. 27	—	5 8	—	34.10	24.10
Aug. 28	—	—	5 5	34. 2	24. 6
1808 Feb. 26	—	—	5 3	34. 6	23. 6
Aug. 26	—	—	5 5	35. 2	23.16
1809 Feb. 28	4 10 0 F	—	5 3	31. 0	20.19
Aug. 22	—	—	5 5½	29. 4	20. 1
1810 Feb. 27	—	—	5 6	29. 0	19.16
Aug. 28	—	—	5 8½	30. 9	21. 6
1811 Feb. 26	4 13 6 F	—	5 11	25. 0	17.16
Aug. 30	4 17 6 F	6 2	6 0	25. 6	18. 2
1812 Feb. 28	4 15 0	—	6 1	28. 0	19.16
Aug. 28	—	—	6 3½	28. 9	19. 5
1813 Feb. 26	—	—	6 6	30. 0	20.80
Aug. 27	—	—	7 0	26. 6	18.80
1814 Feb. 22	5 8 0	6 11½	—	29. 0	21. 0
Aug. 23	4 11 0 F	5 8½	—	32. 0	22.80
1815 Feb. 28	4 9 0	5 11½	5 10	32. 2	22. 0
Aug. 25	—	—	5 7	32. 6	22. 0
1816 Feb. 27	4 2 0	5 4	5 3	34. 8	24.60
Aug. 27	3 19 0	—	4 10½	36. 9	25.80
1817 Feb. 28	3 18 6	5 1	4 11	36. 7	25.40
Aug. 22	4 0 6	—	5 2	35. 0	24.30
1818 Feb. 27	—	5 4½	5 5	34. 0	24. 0
Aug. 25	—	—	5 5	34. 6	24.35
1819 Feb. 19	4 1 0	5 7	5 7	33.11	23.85
Aug. 3	3 18	5 2	—	35.11	25.10
					25.20

CPSIA information can be obtained
at www.ICGtesting.com
Printed in the USA
LVHW010745291118
598533LV00024BA/1316